WORLD STARS

THE ROAD TO THE
WORLD'S MOST POPULAR
CUP:

HISTORY OF THE CUP

MAKING THE FINAL 32

TEAM USA

TOP TEAMS

WORLD STARS

WORLD STARS

MASON CREST

MASON CREST

450 Parkway Drive, Suite D I Broomall, Pennsylvania 19008
(866) MCP-BOOK (toll-free)

Andrew Luke

First printing
9 8 7 6 5 4 3 2 1

ISBN (hardback) 978-1-4222-3950-6
ISBN (series) 978-1-4222-3949-0
ISBN (ebook) 978-1-4222-7828-4

Cataloging-in-Publication Data on file
with the Library of Congress

QR CODES AND LINKS TO THIRD-PARTY CONTENT

You may gain access to certain third-party content ("Third-Party Sites") by scanning and using the QR Codes that appear in this publication (the "QR Codes"). We do not operate or control in any respect any information, products, or services on such Third-Party Sites linked to by us via the QR Codes included in this publication, and we assume no responsibility for any materials you may access using the QR Codes. Your use of the QR Codes may be subject to terms, limitations, or restrictions set forth in the applicable terms of use or otherwise established by the owners of the Third-Party Sites. Our linking to such Third-Party Sites via the QR Codes does not imply an endorsement or sponsorship of such Third-Party Sites or the information, products, or services offered on or through the Third-Party Sites, nor does it imply an endorsement or sponsorship of this publication by the owners of such Third-Party Sites.

CONTENTS

KEY ICONS TO LOOK FOR:

Words to Understand: These words with their easy-to-understand definitions will increase the reader's understanding of the text while building vocabulary skills.

Sidebars: This boxed material within the main text allows readers to build knowledge, gain insights, explore possibilities, and broaden their perspectives by weaving together additional information to provide realistic and holistic perspectives.

Educational videos: Readers can view videos by scanning our QR codes, providing them with additional educational content to supplement the text. Examples include news coverage, moments in history, speeches, iconic sports moments, and much more!

Text-Dependent Questions: These questions send the reader back to the text for more careful attention to the evidence presented there.

Research Projects: Readers are pointed toward areas of further inquiry connected to each chapter. Suggestions are provided for projects that encourage deeper research and analysis.

Series Glossary of Key Terms: This back-of-the book glossary contains terminology used throughout this series. Words found here increase the reader's ability to read and comprehend higher-level books and articles in this field.

Aggregate: combined score of matches between two teams in a two-match (with each often referred to as "legs") format, typically with each team playing one home match.

Away goals rule: tie-breaker applied in some competitions with two-legged matches. In cases where the aggregate score is tied, the team that has scored more goals away from home is deemed the winner.

Cap: each appearance by a player for his national team is referred to as a cap, a reference to an old English tradition where players would all receive actual caps.

Challenge: common term for a tackle—the method of a player winning the ball from an opponent—executed when either running at, beside, or sliding at the opponent.

Clean sheet: referencing no marks being made on the score sheet, when a goalkeeper or team does not concede a single goal during a match; a shutout.

Derby: match between two, usually local, rivals; e.g., Chelsea and Arsenal, both of which play in London.

Dummy: skill move performed by a player receiving a pass from a teammate; the player receiving the ball will intentionally allow the ball to run by them to a teammate close by without touching it, momentarily confusing the opponent as to who is playing the ball.

Equalizer: goal that makes the score even or tied.

First touch: refers to the initial play on a ball received by a player.

Football: a widely used name for soccer. Can also refer to the ball.

Group of death: group in a cup competition that is unusually competitive because the number of strong teams in the group is greater than the number of qualifying places available for the next phase of the tournament.

Kit: soccer-specific clothing worn by players, consisting at the minimum of a shirt, shorts, socks, specialized footwear, and (for goalkeepers) specialized gloves.

Loan: when a player temporarily plays for a club other than the one they are currently contracted to. Such a loan may last from a few weeks to one or more seasons.

Marking: defensive strategy that is either executed man-to-man or by zone, where each player is responsible for a specific area on the pitch.

Match: another word for game.

One touch: style of play in which the ball is passed around quickly using just one touch.

One-two: skill move in which Player One passes the ball to Player Two and runs past the opponent, whereupon they immediately receive the ball back from Player Two in one movement. Also known as a *give-and-go*.

Pitch: playing surface for a game of soccer; usually a specially prepared grass field. Referred to in the Laws of the Game as the field of play.

Set piece: dead ball routine that the attacking team has specifically practiced, such as a free kick taken close to the opposing goal, or a corner kick.

Through-ball: pass from the attacking team that goes straight through the opposition's defense to a teammate who runs to the ball.

Touch line: markings along the side of the pitch, indicating the boundaries of the playing area. Throw-ins are taken from behind this line.

Youth system (academy): young players are contracted to the club and trained to a high standard with the hope that some will develop into professional players. Some clubs provide academic as well as soccer education.

2014 FIFA World Cup champions Germany

Year after year, they are the pillars of their European club teams. From Barcelona and Real Madrid to Manchester City and Bayern Munich, the rosters of Europe's top clubs are headlined by the biggest stars in the sport from around the world. Every four years, these players switch allegiance, trading club responsibility for national pride to represent their countries in the planet's greatest sporting tournament: the FIFA World Cup.

The Fédération Internationale de Football Association, or FIFA, is the governing body for international soccer. Based in Switzerland, FIFA sanctions 10 international tournaments around the world from the under-15 level to beach soccer. The crown jewel of its tournaments, however, is the men's World Cup. Held every four years, this tournament to decide international soccer supremacy is arguably the biggest sporting event in the world.

It is on the World Cup stage that the stars of the sport cement their legends. Success in the world's most watched sporting event can make an ordinary career great and a great career immortal. Names like Rossi, Maradona, Romário, Ronaldo, Zidane, and Messi are among those who have won the title of best player at the World Cup finals, winning the Golden Ball award. Under the sport's biggest spotlight, the biggest stars shine brightest.

Today, the World Cup is more competitive than ever, with more countries competing to qualify than at any time before. More than 200 nations competed to be among the 32 that make the 2018 World Cup final. Soccer's supremely skilled superstars, players that compete at a level above the rest when the time comes to make a play, lead the countries that are the favorites to win.

Whether it is an electrifying run down the touch line by a winger, a deft finish in the box from a striker, a brilliant through ball from a midfielder to create a scoring chance, a defender dispossessing an opponent, or a diving save by a goalkeeper, great players make great plays from every position. *World Stars* takes a look at the best of the best players to compete in the World Cup.

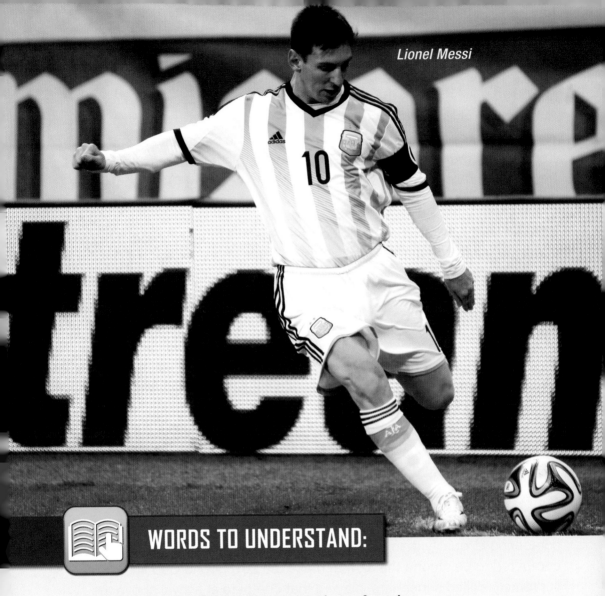

Lionel Messi

WORDS TO UNDERSTAND:

accolade: an award or an expression of praise

archipelago: an expanse of water with many scattered islands

nemesis: a formidable and usually victorious rival or opponent

quibble: to argue or complain about small, unimportant things

CHAPTER 1

WHO'S NUMBER ONE?

In the following chapters of this book, readers may **quibble** with some of the players chosen as the best versus those who have been left out.

In this current chapter, however, few that follow the game of soccer would argue that the choice of who is the number one soccer player in the world comes down to just two players: Argentina's Lionel Messi and Portugal's Cristiano Ronaldo.

Lionel Messi plays as a forward on Argentina's national team (known as the Albiceleste), making his first appearance for them in 2005 at age 18 during an exhibition match (a friendly) against Hungary. He scored his first goal for Argentina seven months later against Croatia, right before the 2006 World Cup in Germany.

Along with Argentina's Lionel Messi, Cristiano Ronaldo of Portugal is considered to be one of the two best soccer players in the world

Messi turned 19 during that World Cup tournament, making his World Cup debut against Serbia and Montenegro eight days prior to his birthday. He scored his first World Cup goal in that match, 13 minutes after coming on as a substitute in the 75th minute. It was the sixth goal in a 6–0 win for Argentina. Messi made his first World Cup start in the next match, the last in the group stage against the Netherlands. He came on as a late substitute in the first match of the knockout stage, a 2–1 win over Mexico, but did not play in the quarterfinal elimination loss to host Germany.

The magic of Messi's dazzling footwork is summarized here

By the time of the 2010 World Cup in South Africa, Messi had emerged as an international superstar. He had been named FIFA World Player of the Year in 2009, which led to a new contract with his club team in Barcelona worth more than $16 million annually. At the World Cup, Javier Mascherano was Argentina's captain, but Messi was one of the team leaders. The team had not played well during qualifying, but nonetheless was expected to do well in the tournament.

The Albiceleste did not disappoint in the group stage, going undefeated. Argentina faced Mexico in its first match of the knockout stage, and won 3–1, with Messi assisting on the opening goal. Argentina was once again eliminated by Germany in the quarterfinals, a decent result for what was considered to be an average team.

Looking to improve upon these disappointing international results, Argentina hired Alejandro Sabella as manager in August 2011. Sabella immediately secured an agreement with Mascherano to transfer the captaincy to Messi. This change in leadership and responsibility was a launching board for Messi. In 2012, he scored a team record of 12 goals in just nine matches. During qualifying for the 2014 World Cup, he scored another 10 goals in 14 matches.

Messi was now considered by many to be the top player in the world.

He had won this very award from FIFA four straight times (2009–12), and entered the 2014 World Cup in Brazil determined to demonstrate his greatness. Messi wasted no time, scoring the winning goal in Argentina's opening match of the World Cup against Bosnia and Herzegovina. He also scored the only goal of the following match, a 1–0 win over Iran. Messi added two more goals in a 3–2 win to close out the group stage against Nigeria.

Messi has been voted as FIFA's top player in the world five times

The Man of the Match is an award given to the player judged to have had the most significant positive impact on each match. This is most often a player on the winning side, and tends to be either a goalkeeper or a goal scorer.

At the World Cup, the Man of the Match award has been given for each match of the tournament since the 2002 event in Japan and South Korea. Experts from FIFA picked the winners until 2010, when FIFA turned to online fan voting to determine the selections. Here are the top winners of the award in their World Cup careers.

Player	Country	World Cup 2002	World Cup 2006	World Cup 2010	World Cup 2014
Arjen Robben	Netherlands		2	1	3
Lionel Messi	Argentina			1	4
Miroslav Klose	Germany	2	2		
Thomas Müller	Germany			2	2
Cristiano Ronaldo	Portugal			3	1
Wesley Sneijder	Netherlands			4	

Argentina's first match in the knockout stage came against Switzerland, during which Messi assisted the only goal and was named Man of the Match for the fourth consecutive time. The Albiceleste continued to play well behind their captain, beating Belgium 1–0 in the quarterfinal. The semifinal match against the Netherlands was 0–0 after 120 minutes, requiring a penalty kick shootout to determine a winner. Messi scored the first penalty for Argentina in winning the shootout 4–2.

With brilliant displays of skill and determination, Messi had led Argentina to the World Cup final, where they would face recent **nemesis** Germany. The Germans had knocked Messi and Argentina out of the last two World Cups. This was the third matchup between the two countries in a World Cup final match, which is a record. They beat the Germans in 1986 and lost to them in 1990.

In the final match, the Germans dominated possession of the ball and put seven shots on target to Argentina's two. Messi missed on a dangerous chance inside the penalty area early in the second half. With no goals scored at the end of regulation time, 30 minutes of extra time was required, and in the 113th minute, Germany finally scored after having several chances. In the final minute, Messi sailed a free kick over the bar in Argentina's last chance to tie the game and Germany won 1–0.

Messi ended the World Cup with four goals and an assist, and was awarded the Golden Ball as the best player in the tournament. He was also named to the FIFA Dream Team, an all-star team selected by fans through an online survey.

Messi was named captain of the Argentina national team in 2011

GOALS

LEAGUE	360
CLUB	522
INTERNATIONAL	61

0 100 200 300 400 500 600

GOALS PER MATCH

LEAGUE **.92**   CLUB **.88**   INTERNATIONAL **.5**

CHAMPIONSHIPS

LEAGUE CHAMPIONSHIP - 8

NATIONAL CHAMPIONSHIP - 4

EUROPEAN CLUB CHAMPIONSHIP - 4

FIFA CLUB WORLD CUP - 3

#10

LIONEL MESSI

2009   **2010**   **2011**

MESSI

FIFA BEST PLAYER IN THE WORLD AWARDS

RONALDO

2008

GOALS

LEAGUE	373
CLUB	535
INTERNATIONAL	79

0   100   200   300   400   500   600

GOALS PER MATCH

LEAGUE **.76**   CLUB **.74**   INTERNATIONAL **.54**

CHAMPIONSHIPS

LEAGUE CHAMPIONSHIP - 5

NATIONAL CHAMPIONSHIP - 3

EUROPEAN CLUB CHAMPIONSHIP - 4

FIFA CLUB WORLD CUP - 3

CRISTIANO RONALDO

#7

2012   2015

2013   2014   2016   2017

Since 2008, the only player to be named best in the world by FIFA other than Messi is Portugal's Cristiano Ronaldo. Ronaldo, who is two years older, won in 2008, 2013, 2014, 2016 and 2017, with Messi winning the other five years.

Ronaldo was born in the **archipelago** of Madeira, which lies about 600 miles southwest of mainland Portugal. He grew up playing locally until age 12 when he was signed by Sporting CP, a Primeira Liga club based in the capital, Lisbon. He soon caught the eye of the Portuguese international program and began playing with the under-15 team in 2001. Ronaldo made his first appearance for the senior team in 2003 at age 18 against Kazakhstan.

By the time qualifying came around for the 2006 World Cup, Ronaldo was Portugal's leading scorer. He scored seven goals in the regional qualifying matches

Ronaldo made his first appearance for Portugal's senior national team at age 18

to help Portugal go undefeated to win its group. At the World Cup in Germany, he scored his first World Cup goal on a penalty kick against Iran as Portugal went undefeated in the group stage. Portugal advanced to the quarterfinals against England, where Ronaldo netted the deciding penalty kick in a shootout win. The tournament ended for Portugal in the semifinal, a 1–0 shutout at the hands of France.

Ronaldo was named captain of the national team before a friendly match with Brazil in 2007, and was named permanent captain in July 2008. He electrified crowds with his speed and unmatched dribbling ability, and that year FIFA crowned him best player in the world for the first time.

Uncharacteristically, Ronaldo struggled during qualifying for the 2010 World Cup, where he did not score in 12 matches. Portugal managed to barely qualify for the tournament in South Africa, where he redeemed himself in the group stage. Ronaldo was named Man of the Match in all three group stage contests. The team went unbeaten, but managed just two goalless draws and a 7–0 win, with Ronaldo scoring one goal. Finishing second in the group earned the Portuguese a match against eventual champions Spain, where they were eliminated 1–0.

In the history of Portuguese soccer, no one has made more appearances (also known as caps) than Ronaldo. His 100th cap came during qualifying for the 2014 World Cup in Brazil. Ronaldo also became Portugal's all-time leading goal scorer during this period. Once again, the team struggled in qualifying and needed to win a playoff against Sweden to make the field of 32. Ronaldo played a spectacular match, scoring four goals to secure a spot in the World Cup.

Ronaldo has won the award for best club player in Europe three times

Cristiano Ronaldo's star power has brought him extraordinary wealth and fame, but the global superstar tries hard to give back to the society that has given him so much. In 2015, Ronaldo was named the most charitable athlete in the world, topping the dosomething.org Athletes Gone Good list. Examples of his philanthropy include:

- *Donating $83,000 to pay for a 10-month-old baby's brain operation*
- *Paying a 9-year-old cancer patient's medical expenses*
- *Donating $135,000 to fund a research center at the hospital where his mother was treated for cancer*
- *Funding aid efforts with a nearly $6.5 million donation after an earthquake in Nepal killed over 8,000 people in 2015*
- *Donating the entirety of his more than half a million dollar 2015 UEFA Champions League bonus to charity*
- *Giving blood at least twice a year (which is why he has no tattoos, because getting one would preclude him from doing so) and donating his bone marrow*

Portugal's struggles continued into the group stage at the World Cup, where it lost the first match 4–0 to eventual champion Germany and managed a draw against the USA. This meant Portugal went into the third game hoping they would beat Ghana and that Germany would beat the USA by enough goals to overcome the goal differential tiebreaker. Goal differential is the difference between the number of goals a team has scored and the number it has allowed. Portugal managed a 2–1 win, with Ronaldo scoring the winner. The USA also lost, but only 1–0, so Portugal was eliminated as the USA finished with a better goal differential.

Ronaldo shields the ball from a defender in a friendly match against Ireland

In 2016, Ronaldo had the best international season of his career, scoring 13 times in 13 matches. This included four goals in a 2018 World Cup qualifying match against Andorra, and two more in another qualifier against Latvia.

Neither Messi nor Ronaldo has yet led their country to World Cup glory. Ronaldo has been to the semifinals in 2006, and Messi one step further to the championship match in 2014. Both men have played in the same three World Cups. Messi has scored five goals in his World Cup matches, plus another 18 and counting in World Cup qualifiers. Ronaldo has just three World Cup goals, but another 24 in qualifying. So which player is the best? Fans of each man will passionately argue their favorite's case, and both sides have a very strong argument. Perhaps either player will someday win the World Cup to add that difference-making **accolade** to his résumé finally. For the objective observer, judgment should be reserved until these great careers are over.

TEXT-DEPENDENT QUESTIONS:

1. Who won FIFA's top player award four straight times from 2009–12?

2. Since 2008, who is the only player to be named best in the world by FIFA other than Messi?

3. How many goals did Ronaldo score in a 2018 World Cup qualifying match against Andorra?

RESEARCH PROJECT:

Messi and Ronaldo may be the two best current players and the best of their generation. But what about the previous generation? Who were the Messi and Ronaldo of world soccer 30 years ago? Which two players were most dominant leading into the 1986 World Cup in Mexico?
Research statistics and game reports to write your own report on what the numbers and the experts were saying.

WORDS TO UNDERSTAND:

ensued: to take place afterward or as a result

give and go: a skill move between teammates to move the ball past an opponent (Player One passes the ball to Player Two and runs past the opponent, whereupon Player One immediately receives the ball back from Player Two, who has received, controlled, and passed the ball in one movement)

vertebra: one of the small bones that link together to form the backbone

CHAPTER 2

SOUTH AMERICAN SUPERSTARS

The majority of the world's best players come from Europe. France, Spain, Germany, England, and Italy lead the way in turning out professional players that thrive at the international level. But when it comes to players who excel at putting the ball in the goal—strikers with a scoring touch—South America is the place to look.

Lionel Messi is, of course, Exhibit A, and the Argentine dynamo was examined in the first chapter. Beyond Messi, however, the talent pool in South America is still very deep, starting with three players who have all been Messi's teammates.

Luis Suárez plays with Messi as a striker on the club team FC Barcelona in Spain's top-flight La Liga. Suárez was born in Salto, Uruguay, and has played for the national team there (known as La Celeste) since 2007. Suárez made 28 appearances for La Celeste leading up to the 2010 World Cup in South Africa.

Luis Suárez, seen here in the sky blue Uruguay uniform, has played for the national team since 2007

Suárez had an eventful tournament, to say the least. In the group stage, he had a goal and an assist in three matches. In Uruguay's final match of the group stage, Suárez was named Man of the Match after he headed in the only goal in a 1–0 win over Mexico to send La Celeste to the knockout stage.

Watch Luis Suárez's pivotal moment in the 2010 World Cup

Uruguay faced South Korea in the round of 16, and Suárez had his best match of the tournament. He scored both goals in a 2–1 win. The first opened the scoring after just 8 minutes, with Suárez tapping in a brilliant cross from teammate Diego Forlán. The second was the match winner in the 80th minute, where Suárez banked a shot from the top left edge of the penalty area off of the far post and in. He was named Man of the Match for the second consecutive time.

La Celeste's next match, the quarterfinal against Ghana, is the most famous of Suárez's international career. He did not stand out for his usual offensive brilliance, however. Suárez took center stage with the match tied 1–1 in the 31st minute of extra time. Ghana had won a free kick from the right side, about 5 yards outside the penalty area. John Paintsil of Ghana swung the ball into the area, and a mad scramble **ensued**. With his goalkeeper out of position, Suárez found himself standing on the goal line as Ghana tried desperately to score. He blocked one shot with his left leg, and then famously swatted a second with his left hand.

SIDEBAR: RED CARD

A red card is issued by the referee in two instances in a match. Either a player has committed a very significant foul deserving of immediate removal from the match, or the player has received two yellow card cautions in the match, which equals a red card. In 2016, FIFA amended the rule affecting the first of these instances. It used to be that a foul on a running striker committed by the last man of the defense would result in a direct red card. With the rule change, as long as the foul is judged to be an honest attempt at taking the ball, the defender will only be shown a yellow card, unless the foul is violent or consists of a deliberate hand ball in the box.

Suárez was shown a red card and ejected, and Ghana was awarded a penalty kick. Suárez watched from the tunnel leading to the Uruguay dressing room as Ghana's Asamoah Gyan put the penalty kick off the crossbar. Suárez celebrated on his way down the tunnel, later saying, "I think it was just instinct. Any player would have done the same, not just me." Uruguay went on to win in penalty kicks to advance to the semifinals. "I made the best save of the tournament," Suárez said.

Suárez's international career has not lacked for controversy, including an infamous hand ball at the 2010 World Cup and several instances of biting other players

Without Suárez, Uruguay lost the next match 3–2 to the Netherlands. He returned for the third place game, where he made a beautiful pass to set up Uruguay's first goal against Germany in another 3–2 loss.

Leading up to the 2014 World Cup in Brazil, Suárez was lethal, scoring 11 goals in qualifying. He was recovering from knee surgery at the beginning of the World Cup itself and sat out Uruguay's opening 3–1 loss to Costa Rica. He played the following game, scoring both goals in a 2–1 win over England. In the third match against Italy, controversy found Suárez again, this time in a late second half incident where he bit Italy's Giorgio Chiellini on the shoulder during a challenge for the ball. Uruguay won 1–0 to advance, but Suárez was suspended for nine matches for the biting incident. This was the third time in his career that Suárez had bitten an opponent. Without Suárez, Uruguay was eliminated in the next match against Colombia.

Suárez is the all-time leader in international goals for Uruguay.

No group of great South American players is complete without a representative from Brazil. Neymar da Silva Santos Júnior is better known simply as Neymar. Neymar was born near São Paulo in Brazil in 1992. He grew up playing youth club soccer with top-flight Brazilian club Santos. On the international stage, he began playing for Brazil with the under-17 team. At age 18, he made his debut with the senior team in 2010.

In the run-up to the 2014 World Cup in Brazil, Neymar made more than 45 appearances for his country. As the host nation, Brazil qualified automatically. In the tournament, Brazil drew Group A and opened the World Cup with a match against Croatia in front of Neymar's hometown crowd in São Paulo. He wasted little time in whipping the crowd into a frenzy with a goal in the 29th minute to level the match at 1–1. Neymar then scored the winner by converting a penalty kick midway through the second half. He was named Man of the Match.

After a goalless draw against Mexico in its second match, Brazil faced Cameroon in the third. Neymar once again scored his team's first goal, finishing a cross from Luiz Gustavo. After Cameroon equalized, Neymar again scored the winning goal, this time off of a brilliant run on a **give and go**. Brazil cruised to a 4–1 win and won Group A. Neymar was again named Man of the Match.

Like his idol and fellow countryman Pelé, Neymar da Silva Santos Júnior wears number 10 for Brazil

Brazil faced South American rivals Chile in the round of 16. Following first half goals by each side, Brazil dominated possession, but the match went through extra time to a penalty kick shootout even at 1–1. In the shootout, both teams missed two of their first four penalty kicks. Neymar was selected to take the fifth round kick for Brazil and he scored, forcing Chile to make its kick to prolong the shootout. Gonzalo Jara, however, missed by hitting the post and his team was eliminated.

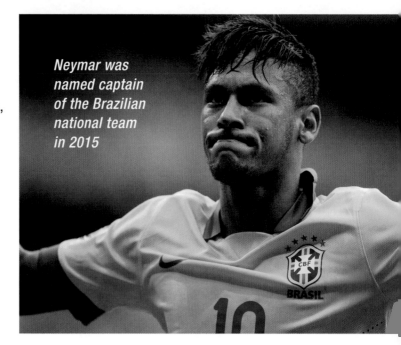

Neymar was named captain of the Brazilian national team in 2015

The quarterfinal match pitted Brazil against another South American opponent, Colombia, and proved to be fateful for Brazil and Neymar. Neymar made his presence felt early, creating a goal by Captain Thiago Silva with a perfect corner kick to the back post. Disaster came late for Brazil, however. With less than 2 minutes remaining in the match and Brazil leading 2–1, Neymar was tackled by Colombian defender Juan Camilo Zúñiga, who struck Neymar in the middle of his back with a knee. The blow fractured Neymar's **vertebra**, and he was unable to play any further in the tournament. Without Neymar and Silva, who was suspended for collecting multiple yellow cards, the Germans humiliated Brazil 7–1 on home soil. Brazil also lost badly to the Dutch in the third place match, 3–0.

Despite missing two of Brazil's matches, Neymar scored four goals and one assist, enough to win the Bronze Boot as the third highest scorer in the tournament. He was also named to the tournament Dream Team.

In 2015, Neymar was voted third best player in the world by FIFA, behind only Messi and Ronaldo. In 2017, Neymar transferred from his club side at Barcelona to Paris Saint-Germain for a world record transfer fee of more than $260 million.

Messi and Sergio Agüero are the offensive weapons for Argentina's national team. Agüero was born in Buenos Aires in 1988, and began playing nationally for Argentina's under-17 team in 2004. He was promoted to the senior team in 2006, and scored his first senior international goal in a qualifying match for the 2010 World Cup against Bolivia. Agüero would score in three other qualifying matches.

At the 2010 World Cup, Agüero was not a starter. He did not play in the Group B opener against Nigeria, but came on as a mid-second half substitute in the second match against South Korea. The score was 2–1 for the Albiceleste at the time.

Sergio Agüero is the third-leading goal scorer in the history of Argentina's national team

Gonzalo Higuaín scored his second goal of the match in the 76th minute, one minute after Agüero came on, to make it 3–1. Four minutes later, Higuaín struck again, this time off a beautiful first touch chip cross from Agüero. Agüero showed enough in 15 minutes to earn a start in the third match against Greece alongside Messi. Argentina won all three matches to win the group. In the knockout stage, Agüero was not used in a win over Mexico, and was a late substitute in the quarterfinal loss against Germany, called on shortly after the Germans scored to go up 3–0.

Leading up to the 2014 World Cup, Agüero scored five goals in eight qualifying matches and was the starter up front alongside Messi.

Agüero was a late substitute in this match against the Netherlands at the 2014 World Cup in Brazil. He later scored a crucial penalty kick to help Argentina win the match in a penalty shootout

Unfortunately, Agüero suffered a thigh injury shortly before the World Cup began. He started but was ineffective in the first two group stage matches. In the first half of the third match against Nigeria, he was unable to continue and was removed from the field. He missed the next two games, returning as a late substitute in the semifinal against the Netherlands. With neither team able to score, the match went to a penalty kick shootout. With the Dutch having missed two of their first three attempts, Agüero was called on to take the third attempt for Argentina, which had been perfect so far. He made the shot, and Argentina won on the next shot to advance. Agüero, clearly limited by his injury, was again a second half substitute in the final match against Germany, which Argentina lost 1–0.

From Pelé to Ronaldo and Di Stéfano to Maradona, South America has produced some of the best strikers that have ever lived. It is no surprise to see players like Suárez, Neymar, and Agüero keeping this tradition alive today.

TEXT-DEPENDENT QUESTIONS:

1. Which five countries lead the way in turning out professional players that thrive at the international level?

2. Who was named Man of the Match in the 2010 World Cup after he headed in the only goal in a 1–0 win over Mexico to send La Celeste to the knockout stage?

3. In 2015, who was voted third best player in the world by FIFA, behind only Messi and Ronaldo?

RESEARCH PROJECT:

South America has always produced great strikers, but are they the best of all time? Do some research comparing the best ever European strikers to the best ever from South America. Pick five players from each continent and compare. Write a report that explains which side you think comes out on top.

WORDS TO UNDERSTAND:

deflection: an action in which the ball suddenly changes direction because it has hit something—often another player

rout: a decisive or disastrous defeat

stifled: to make something difficult or impossible

tallied: to score or make a point

CHAPTER 3

MIDFIELD MAGICIANS

In soccer, strikers get much of the glory. Goals, after all, are rare in the sport, and those that score them are understandably worshiped. The real control of a match, however, comes not from the front line of a team but rather from the center. The game is controlled through midfield, where the most talented of players are able to control possession, moderate the tempo, and create attacks.

The current maestro of the midfield is Spaniard Andrés Iniesta. He was born in a small town in southeastern Spain in 1984. Iniesta began playing for his national junior team with the under-15 squad until he made his first appearance at age 22 for the senior team, known as La Roja, after Spain had already qualified for the 2006 World Cup in Germany.

Andrés Iniesta is revered for his extraordinary passing and ball control ability

Iniesta's first World Cup appearance came in the third match of the group stage against Saudi Arabia. Spain had already secured first place in the group by winning its first two matches, where Iniesta had watched from the bench. With advancement assured, manager Luis Aragonés gave Iniesta the start, resting all three of his regular midfielders. Spain won 1–0. This was Iniesta's only appearance in that World Cup as France eliminated Spain in the next match.

After the tournament, Iniesta returned to his club team at Barcelona, where he had played since 2002. There, along with Messi, he helped Barcelona to its first La Liga title in six years, winning back-to-back in 2005 and 2006. Barcelona also won the UEFA (Union of European Football Associations) Champion's League titles in 2006 and again in 2009. By the time of the 2010 World Cup in South Africa, Iniesta was a seasoned veteran of Spain's national squad.

Iniesta was named Man of the Match in the final match of the 2010 World Cup in South Africa after scoring the tournament-winning goal in extra time

Not known for his goal scoring, Iniesta did score in a World Cup qualifying match against Belgium in 2008. Spain entered the tournament as FIFA's second-ranked team in the world, behind only Brazil. Spain drew into Group H and faced a determined Swiss team in its first match. Iniesta started on left wing in a 1–0 defeat to the Swiss. He injured his thigh in the Swiss match and sat out the second match, a 2–0 win over Honduras.

Spain needed a win in match three against Chile and Iniesta was back in the lineup, this time on right wing. With Spain up 1–0 in the first half, Iniesta scored a second goal for Spain when he ran on to a nice back pass by David Villa to the top of the area. Iniesta's goal turned out to be the winning strike in a 2–1 win that won Spain the group. Iniesta was named Man of the Match.

In the knockout stage, Spain defeated Portugal 1–0 to face Paraguay in the quarterfinals. Iniesta was slotted back into a more natural midfield spot, where he was dominant in controlling the match, putting together more than 50 passes and initiating several of Spain's attacking moves. For his persistent threatening of the Paraguay defenders, Iniesta was named Man of the Match.

In the semifinal, Spain beat Germany 1–0 to make the final against the Netherlands. The final was a close affair, with no team able to score in regulation time. In extra time, the match went into the 116th minute before an attack from Spain resulted in Cesc Fàbregas collecting a **deflection** at the top of the Dutch area and feeding Iniesta on the right for the finish. His goal won him Man of the Match and stood as the one that won the World Cup.

For the 2014 World Cup in Brazil, the top-ranked Spaniards did not have to qualify as they were defending champions. They drew into Group B and faced the Dutch in the opening match. Seeking revenge for their loss in the 2010 final, the Netherlands scored early and often, with three first half goals and two more in the second for a 5–1 win. Spain's tournament turned disastrous in the second match, a 2–0 loss to Chile that eliminated La Roja.

Iniesta is now a World Cup veteran with more than 100 international appearances (caps). Paul Pogba of France is another of the world's great midfielders, one who is just beginning to show how great he could be.

Paul Pogba was named Man of the Match in this round of 16 contest against Nigeria at the 2014 World Cup in Brazil

SIDEBAR: TOP 10 ALL-TIME CAP LEADERS

PLAYER	COUNTRY	CAPS
Ahmed Hassan	Egypt	184
Hossam Hassan	Egypt	178
Claudio Suárez	Mexico	177
Mohamed Al-Deayea	Saudi Arabia	172
Iván Hurtado	Ecuador	168
Gianluigi Buffon*	Italy	173
Iker Casillas*	Spain	167
Vitālijs Astafjevs	Latvia	166
Cobi Jones	United States	164
Mohammed Al-Khilaiwi	Saudi Arabia	163

* - active

Pogba grew up on the outskirts of Paris in the 1990s, catching the attention of junior club Roissy-en-Brie at age 6. By age 15, he was representing the national junior team, and in 2013 at age 20, he debuted for Les Bleus, the senior national team of France.

That first appearance came during qualifying for the 2014 World Cup. Pogba was already a big star in Europe, having moved to Manchester United's youth club in 2009, and starring for United since 2011. He made the French team for the World Cup and had a standout tournament.

In the first French match, Pogba drew a yellow card and played just 57 minutes of the 3–0 win. In the next match, however, Pogba was brilliant in setting up the fourth of five goals against Switzerland in a 5–2 win. The group stage concluded with a 0–0 draw with Ecuador.

The knockout stage began with a match against Nigeria, and Pogba was extremely strong. Late in the second half, in a match where neither team had scored, Pogba capitalized on a French corner kick. The goalkeeper misplayed the ball, which deflected toward Pogba. Pogba made no mistake heading the ball firmly into the goal. He was named Man of the Match.

Pogba was named Best Young Player at the 2014 World Cup in Brazil

The Germans were next up for the French. Germany **stifled** France with tough defense and held on for a 1–0 win. Despite being eliminated in the quarterfinals, Pogba was still awarded the Best Young Player award for the tournament.

Two years prior to the World Cup, Pogba had left Manchester United for Juventus in Italy's Serie A. In 2016, after four consecutive league titles at Juventus, he transferred back to United for a record transfer fee of $117 million. Known for his outrageous hairstyles and his creative play, the electrifying 25-year-old Frenchman's best years are still ahead of him.

At 28 years old, German central midfielder Toni Kroos is a veteran of two World Cup teams. Born in Greifswald in January 1990, Kroos started playing for the local youth team at age 7, eventually working his way up to the youth team for Bayern Munich, the top team in Germany's top-flight Bundesliga, at age 16. He was 15 when he debuted with the national under-17 club. At 17, he played his first match with the senior Bayern Munich squad, and at 20, he debuted with the senior national team.

Kroos is known for his playmaking ability and skill at set pieces. As one of the younger players on the squad at the 2010 World Cup in South Africa, the chances for him to demonstrate his skills were limited. In Group D play, Kroos watched the first two matches, a win against Australia and a shocking loss to Serbia, from the bench. He debuted as a late substitute in the third match against Ghana, which Germany won 1–0 to advance.

ut stage, Kroos did not play in Germany's win over
came on late in the 4–0 quarterfinal win over Argentina
me all but secured. He also played 28 minutes in the 1–0
to Spain and 10 minutes in the third-place match victory

Paul Pogba of France and Toni Kroos of Germany met in the quarterfinals of the 2014 World Cup in Brazil. A Kroos set piece resulted in the match-winning goal for the Germans

In 2012, Kroos asserted himself as a starter on the national team as his reputation as a Bundesliga star continued to grow. During qualifying for the 2014 World Cup in Brazil, Kroos scored twice in a 5–0 **rout** of Ireland, and added another goal in a September 2013 qualifier against Austria as Germany went undefeated in qualifying.

Germany entered the 2014 World Cup as FIFA's second-ranked team in the world behind Spain, and opened as the heavy favorites to win Group G. Opening against a Ronaldo-led Portuguese team, Kroos and the Germans made a statement with a dominating 4–0 win. Kroos set up the second goal by executing a sweeping corner kick to the head of teammate Mats Hummels. Germany went on to win the group and advance to the knockout stage.

The Germans opened against Algeria in a tight match that was scoreless through regulation time. Germany scored both early and late during extra time to win 2–1 and reach the quarterfinals against France.

Against the French, Kroos again created a goal out of a set piece, this time on a free kick again headed in by Hummels. That proved to be the lone goal of the match as Germany advanced to the semifinals.

Toni Kroos and Germany dismantle Brazil at the 2014 World Cup

The semifinal opponent was host nation Brazil, and Kroos had his best match of the tournament. Thomas Müller converted a Kroos corner from the right side in the 11th minute to open the scoring. A Kroos attack up the middle led to the second goal, and then, already ahead 2–0, Kroos shockingly scored goals 2 minutes apart. The first came on a cross from Philipp Lahm right to the feet of Müller. With everyone expecting a shot from Müller, the Brazilians were caught off guard when Müller missed the ball and it bounced through to a wide-open Kroos on the left, who

Kroos dribbles away from Argentina's Lionel Messi in the final match of the 2014 World Cup in Brazil. Kroos and Germany won 1–0

easily **tallied** with his left foot. Two minutes later, Kroos stripped the ball from a Brazilian defender 27 yards out and initiated a give and go with Sami Khedira that easily eluded the lone remaining defender and the goalkeeper. Khedira scored himself 3 minutes later to make it 5–0, as Germany won easily 7–1. Kroos was honored as the FIFA Man of the Match.

Germany went on to defeat Messi and Argentina 1–0 to win the World Cup. Kroos was nominated for the Golden Ball (ultimately won by Messi) and was named to the FIFA Dream Team for the tournament. FIFA's World Cup Index, which uses tracking technology to evaluate player performance, rated Kroos as the top performer of the tournament. His four assists were the most of any player in the tournament.

Honorable mention among the midfielders goes to Belgium's Eden Hazard, an attacking midfielder and dazzling playmaker. Along with Kroos, Pogba, and Iniesta, they are the best field generals in the world, dictating play and driving the success of their teams.

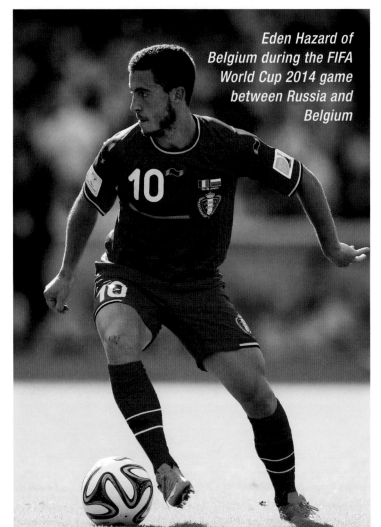

Eden Hazard of Belgium during the FIFA World Cup 2014 game between Russia and Belgium

TEXT-DEPENDENT QUESTIONS:

1. Which player is now a World Cup veteran with more than 100 international appearances?

2. Who caught the attention of junior club Roissy-en-Brie at age 6?

3. FIFA's World Cup Index rated Kroos as the top performer of which tournament?

RESEARCH PROJECT:

This chapter discusses the best current midfielders in the sport, but who were the best midfielders ever to play the game? Do the research to write a report on the top five players in the history of the position, including stats, style of play, and explain why you think they were the best.

WORDS TO UNDERSTAND:

floundered: to have a lot of problems and difficulties

mainstay: a very important part of something; something or someone that provides support and makes it possible for something to exist or succeed

tuberculosis: a serious disease that mainly affects the lungs

CHAPTER 4

THE DEFENDERS

High-level soccer is primarily a defensive game. Teams tend to focus much more on strategies that prevent opponents from scoring rather than on scoring goals themselves. In order to succeed, teams must be sound at the back. Good defenders are essential for good teams.

Spain's Sergio Ramos is one of the world's best defenders. Ramos was born in 1986 near Seville in southern Spain, and grew up playing youth soccer for Sevilla, the local club team, at age 10. His play in the Sevilla youth program got Ramos national recognition, and he began playing with the national program on the under-17 team in 2002. In 2005, Ramos made his debut with the senior national team four days before his 19th birthday.

In October 2005, Ramos scored his first two international goals in a qualifying match for the 2006 World Cup against San Marino. Spain was undefeated in qualifying and entered the World Cup in Germany ranked 5th in the world. The Spaniards drew into Group H with the 20-year-old Ramos as the starting right back. Spain cruised through the group stage, giving up just one goal in its three wins, but lost 3–1 to France in the next round.

Check out this compilation of the skills of Sergio Ramos

Led by Ramos, Spain entered the 2010 World Cup ranked behind only Brazil, and were favored by many to win the tournament. Things started shakily as Spain lost 1–0 to Switzerland in its first match. Spain secured the group, however, with wins in its next two games.

In the first match of the knockout stage, Spain battled Ronaldo and Portugal to a 1–0 win to set up a quarterfinal match against Paraguay. Spain recorded yet another clean sheet, beating Paraguay 1–0. Ramos and the Spanish defense had allowed only two goals in five matches.

Sergio Ramos was named captain of the Spanish National team in 2016

In the semifinals against Germany, it was more of the same, as the stifling defense kept the Germans bottled up and Spain recorded its third consecutive 1–0 win. In the final match against the Netherlands, neither team was able to score until 26 minutes into extra time, when Iniesta famously scored the winner.

Ramos was named to the FIFA Dream Team for the tournament. FIFA's World Cup Index rated him as the top performer of the tournament.

SIDEBAR: FIFA'S WORLD CUP INDEX

During every World Cup tournament since 2010, FIFA has tracked the performance of each player on the field using a system of mathematical formulas to analyze data. As FIFA describes it, they use "the latest FIFA tracking technology to capture data on each player, which will then be analyzed by a team of Performance Analysts. Every pass, tackle and move on the field is measured and assessed to see if it has a positive or negative impact on a team's ability to score or concede a goal. The team of Performance Analysts crunch all the data to award each player an Index score out of 10— the stronger the player's performance, the higher their score."

A 2–0 loss in this group stage match against Chile eliminated Ramos and Spain from the 2014 World Cup in Brazil

For the 2014 World Cup in Brazil, the defending champions drew into a group with Chile (ranked 14th), the Netherlands (ranked 15th), and the lowest-ranked team in the tournament, Australia (ranked 62nd), and were favored to win the group. The tournament, however, proved to be a disaster for La Roja.

Spain opened against the Dutch and had a 1–0 lead late in the first half when it allowed a 44th-minute goal to Dutch star Robin van Persie. The wheels came off for the Spaniards in the second half, as goalkeeper Iker Casillas struggled, allowing four more Dutch goals. The 5–1 loss was the worst ever by a defending champion.

Spain could not recover from the embarrassment against the Netherlands. La Roja allowed two first half goals and lost 2–0 to Chile in the next match. The defeat to Chile eliminated Ramos and his team.

Ramos was named captain for the Euro 2016, the European championship tournament held every four years, where Spain lost in the round of 16. He has continued to captain the squad through qualifying for the 2018 World Cup in Russia.

For Brazil's Thiago Silva, his soccer career was nearly over before it truly began. At 20 years old, the native of Rio de Janeiro was diagnosed

A bout of tuberculosis nearly ended Thiago Silva's career at age 20

with **tuberculosis** while attempting to catch on with the Dynamo Moscow club in Russia. Silva's career had **floundered** after leaving his native Brazil for Europe in 2004. Battling the symptoms of his yet-to-be-diagnosed illness, Silva had failed to catch on with a senior team in Portugal. It was the doctors in Moscow who finally determined what was wrong, and treatment turned into a six-month hospital stay. His mother Angela had to convince Silva not to quit the sport.

In 2006, Silva returned home and attempted a comeback with Fluminense, a Brazilian Série A club whose youth program he had played for briefly when he was 14. His career blossomed again at Fluminense, where Silva's dominant play drew the attention of the national team program, which invited him to try out for the 2008 Olympic team for the Beijing games. There, he played in just two matches as Brazil captured a bronze medal. Brazilian manager Dunga was reluctant to use him in his lineup despite all the success Silva was having on the club level, where Silva had moved to A.C. Milan, a Serie A club in Italy.

Silva was the anchor of the Milan defense that won the Serie A title in 2010–11, winning both Milan Player of the Season and Serie A Player of the Season. Despite this, Dunga refused to play Silva during the 2010 World Cup, so the defender sat on the bench the entire tournament. Dunga was fired after Brazil's loss in the quarterfinals. New manager Mano Menezes not only played Silva, but also named him captain.

Despite a silver medal at the 2012 Olympics, Brazil continued to struggle, and Luiz Felipe Scolari replaced Menezes as manager. Silva, on the other hand, continued to thrive at the club level, transferring from Milan to the top French club Paris St.-Germain for $54 million. In 2013, Silva led Brazil to a win at the FIFA Confederation's Cup in Brazil, and Scolari and Brazil hoped to harness some of his success for the 2014 World Cup, also on home soil.

At the World Cup, Brazil won Group A with Silva as captain and playing every minute at center back. In the round of 16 match against Chile, it was a touch from Silva that set up the opening goal by David Luiz. Brazil won in a penalty shootout after the match was still tied 1–1 following extra time.

SIDEBAR: SOCCER IN THE OLYMPICS

Soccer has been a part of the modern Summer Olympic Games since the second event in Paris in 1900. That tournament included just three countries and was won by Great Britain. In St. Louis in 1904, there were again just three teams, but this time from only two countries: one from Canada and two American teams. The Canadians won.

Today, the Olympic tournament boasts 16 teams that battle to qualify to play on the Olympic stage (the host nation receives an automatic berth). Unlike the World Cup, players must be under 23 years of age. Teams are, however, each permitted to have up to three overage players.

The most success in Olympic competition has been achieved by a non-traditional soccer nation, Hungary. The Hungarians have won five medals, including three gold. All were won in 1972 or before. Great Britain has also won three gold medals, but none since 1912. Unsurprisingly, Brazil has won the most medals, with six. But what is surprising about this is that the only gold in the total was finally won just in 2016, on home soil.

The semifinal against Colombia was momentous for Silva and Brazil. Silva scored in the 7th minute off a corner kick by Neymar. In the 64th minute, however, Silva picked up a yellow card, his second of the tournament. This meant he was automatically suspended for the next match. In the 88th minute, Neymar was injured and would also miss the next match. Brazil won 2–1, but without Silva and Neymar, they were humiliated 7–1 by Germany in the semifinal. Silva was selected for the FIFA Dream Team.

Dunga replaced Scolari as manager after the World Cup and stripped Silva's captaincy, naming Neymar in his place. Dunga then dropped Silva from the team following the 2015 Copa America tournament. Brazil performed poorly under Dunga and without Silva. Dunga was fired again in June of 2016, a year after dropping Silva. New manager Tite immediately called Silva and reinstated him for the 2018 World Cup qualifying campaign.

Mats Hummels and his German teammates are on a quest to defend the World Cup at the 2018 tournament in Russia. Hummels got his start in the Bayern Munich youth system at age 6. Despite 13 years in the

Mats Hummels was a finalist for the Golden Ball award for best player at the 2014 World Cup in Brazil

Bayern system, he only played one match for the senior club before being sent to Bundesliga rivals Borussia Dortmund in 2008. Hummels, a big, powerful center back at 6'3", was already on the national team radar at this point, having played several matches for the under-21 squad. In May of 2010, he debuted for the senior national team, but did not make the 2010 World Cup team in South Africa. He continued to improve, however, and by 2012 Hummels was a **mainstay** on the German defense, playing every second of Euro 2012. Germany qualified as the second-ranked team for the 2014 World Cup in Brazil and was one of the favorites to win.

Germany drew into Group G, where the opening match was against Cristiano Ronaldo and fourth-ranked Portugal. Germany and Hummels foreshadowed the tournament they would have by dominating Ronaldo and the Portuguese. Hummels scored the second German goal in a 4–0 win by heading in a corner kick.

After a surprising draw against Ghana in the second match, Germany faced the USA needing only a draw to advance in match three. The Germans managed to win 1–0 to secure the group, moving on to face Algeria, where they needed extra time to win 2–1.

In the quarterfinal against France, Hummels again showed his value on set pieces when he won a battle for position against a French defender to head in a free kick. Hummels's early marker proved to be the only goal of the match.

Germany went on to famously dismantle an undermanned Brazil 7–1 in the semifinals, and then won the World Cup with a hard fought 1–0 victory over Messi and Argentina.

After the tournament, Hummels was named as a finalist for the Golden Ball award as the tournament's best player (Messi won the award). He was also named to the FIFA

Hummels battles for the ball in a quarterfinal match against France
at the 2014 World Cup in Brazil.
Hummels scored the only goal of the match.

Dream Team and was the fourth-ranked player on the FIFA World Cup Index.

In Euro 2016, Germany played strongly, going through to the quarterfinals against Italy. Late in the match, Hummels picked up his second yellow card of the tournament, meaning he would be suspended for the semifinals should Germany advance. Hummels helped to secure the win against Italy by making a penalty kick in the shootout. Without Hummels, however, and other key players like Khedira and an injured Jérôme Boateng, Germany lost 2–0 to France in the semis.

Hummels, Ramos, and Silva will all likely be mainstays in the center of their respective countries' defenses in the 2018 World Cup, all of them past champions intent on adding another trophy to their collection.

TEXT-DEPENDENT QUESTIONS:

1. Name one of the world's best defenders from Spain.

2. At age 20, which player was diagnosed with tuberculosis?

3. After the 2014 World Cup, Hummels was named as a finalist for the Golden Ball award as the tournament's best player, but lost to which player?

RESEARCH PROJECT:

This chapter discusses the best current defenders in the sport, but who were the best ever to play the game? Do the research to write a report on the top five players in the history of the position, including stats, style of play, and explain why you think they were the best.

boast: to talk with excessive pride and self-satisfaction about one's achievements, possessions, or abilities

consensus: a general agreement about something; an idea or opinion that is shared by all the people in a group

faltered: to stop being strong or successful; to begin to fail or weaken

CHAPTER 5

MANUEL NEUER AND THE REST OF THE GOALIES

If there is any **consensus** on who is the best player in the world at any position, it is that Manuel Neuer at goalkeeper is it. Even Messi has Ronaldo (or the other way around, if you prefer), but Neuer has no rival.

Neuer grew up near Essen in western Germany. He entered the youth program of Bundesliga club Schalke at age 6, and at age 20, he debuted with the senior club. He was also playing for the national program youth teams by then.

In May of 2009, Neuer made his debut for the German senior team at age 23. By the following year, Neuer had become the number one goalkeeper for sixth-ranked Germany entering the 2010 World Cup in South Africa.

Neuer was brilliant in the group stage, allowing just a single goal to Serbia as Germany won Group A. Germany advanced to play England in the round of 16, and Neuer made a key play to open the scoring. He launched one of his patented free goal kicks to a streaking Miroslav Klose, who ran behind the English defense to volley the ball past the keeper on its second bounce. Germany won 4–1.

In the quarterfinals against Argentina, Neuer posted a clean sheet as Germany won easily, 4–0. The semifinal against a powerful Spanish side, led by Ramos and Iniesta, proved more challenging. La Roja controlled much of the match, taking nearly three times as many shot attempts and forcing Neuer to make four saves. In the 73rd minute, Spain finally beat him off a corner kick and won 1–0.

After the World Cup, Neuer returned to Schalke. He was named captain for the 2010–11 season, in which he led the club to the DFB-Pokal, the German national championship. At the end of the season, he signed with Bayern Munich, who paid about $30 million. He started his career at Bayern with a bang, setting a record by going more than 1,000 minutes without allowing a goal.

Manuel Neuer is considered to be the best goalkeeper in the world, and some argue he is the best player at any position. In 2014, Neuer finished third behind Messi and Ronaldo in voting for FIFA's best player in the world

For the national team, Neuer dominated as well, winning all 10 qualifying matches for Euro 2012. Germany went unbeaten in group play, with Neuer allowing two goals in three matches. In the round of 16, he allowed two goals to Greece, although one was a penalty kick. The Germans **faltered** in the semifinals, losing 2–1 to Italy.

The stage was set for the second-ranked Germans at the 2014 World Cup in Brazil. As expected, they came out strong in the opener against Portugal, and Neuer posted a clean sheet in a 4–0 win. In the second match against Ghana, the German defense did not play well, giving Neuer little chance on two goals in a 2–2 draw. He responded by posting a clean sheet against the USA for a 1–0 win that also won the group.

In the round of 16, the match against Algeria went to extra time scoreless, and Neuer was not beaten until right before the final whistle in the 121st minute with Germany up 2–0. Neuer then posted a clean sheet against France in the quarterfinals and made seven saves against the host Brazilians in a 7–1 semifinals win. Neuer capped off a brilliant tournament with 120 scoreless minutes against Argentina, as Germany scored in extra time for the 1–0 win.

Neuer won the Golden Glove award as the top goalkeeper in the tournament and was named the FIFA Dream Team goalkeeper. That year, Neuer finished third in the voting for FIFA's best player in the world, behind only Ronaldo and Messi, which is unprecedented for a goalkeeper.

After leading Germany to a semifinal appearance at Euro 2016, Neuer was named team captain. He holds records for most clean sheets in a Bundesliga season and fastest to 100 clean sheets in Bundesliga history.

Check out this comparison video between Manuel Neuer and Gianluigi Buffon

While no current goalkeeper can compare to Neuer, the German will be thankful to **boast** a career similar to that of Italy's Gianluigi Buffon someday. Buffon is eight years older than Neuer and has played more than 20 seasons at the top levels of the sport.

Buffon was born in Tuscany and played his youth soccer in the Parma system starting at age 13. He made Parma's Serie A club at age 17,

Neuer kept a clean sheet in this quarterfinal win over France

Italy's Gianluigi Buffon holds dozens of goalkeeping records, including fewest goals allowed at a World Cup (2)

two years before his debut with the national senior team. No Italian has played more matches for his country than Buffon.

His first appearance came in October of 1997, during qualifications for the 1998 World Cup in France. Buffon made the World Cup team as the second goalie but did not play a minute behind Gianluca Pagliuca.

Buffon took over as the starter in 2000, the same year he played his last season at Parma. In 2001, he moved to Juventus for a goalkeeper record fee of more than $47 million.

In 2002, Buffon led the sixth-ranked Italians into the 2002 World Cup in Japan and South Korea. The Italians played poorly in a group stage loss to Croatia, and advanced out of Group G in second place. This resulted in a matchup against South Korea in the next round. Buffon saved a penalty in regulation time, but Italy lost the match on a late goal in extra time.

Redemption came for Buffon in 2006 at the World Cup final tournament in Germany. The Italians drew into a difficult Group E, with the Czechs (ranked 2nd) and the Americans (ranked 5th) both ranking above number 13 Italy. Italy opened against the other team in the group, Ghana, and Buffon kept a clean sheet in a 2–0 win. His own teammate beat Buffon in the second match against the USA: an own goal by Cristian Zaccardo resulted in a 1–1 draw. Buffon kept another clean sheet in a 2–0 win against the Czechs to win the group.

In the knockout stage, Buffon continued to be unbeatable, with clean sheets in the second round against Australia (Buffon was Man of the Match), the quarterfinals against Ukraine, and the semifinals against host country Germany. He finally conceded an actual goal in the final against France, and that came on a penalty kick. Italy won the World Cup in a penalty shootout. In seven matches, Buffon conceded just two goals, which is a World Cup record. The two that beat him: an own goal and a penalty kick.

Buffon won the Yashin award (since renamed the Golden Glove) as best goalkeeper in the tournament, and was named to the FIFA World Cup All-Star Team.

In 2008, Buffon was named as an acting captain behind Fabio Cannavaro, and first served as captain when Cannavaro was injured for the opening match of Euro 2008. In 2010, Italy went to South Africa in defense of its World Cup title, but Buffon played just 45 minutes in the opening match before he was lost to injury for the tournament. Without Buffon, Italy managed just two draws and was eliminated.

In 2011, Cannavaro retired from international play and Buffon was named captain. He led Gli Azzurri, as the team is nicknamed, to a runner-up showing at Euro 2012, but Italy was again eliminated at the group stage in the 2014 World Cup.

If Buffon never wins another World Cup, he has plenty of accolades to fall back on. He holds several club and league records for appearances at Juventus and in Serie A. In 2015–16, he went 974 minutes without conceding a goal in league play, recording 10 straight clean sheets. He has been named Serie A Goalkeeper of the Year a record 11 times.

SIDEBAR: PENALTY SHOOTOUT

In the knockout phase of tournaments, or in multi-leg competitions where the score is tied following both regulation and extra time, a winner is determined by the penalty shootout. Each team elects five different players to take a penalty kick against the opposing goalkeeper. The teams take turns shooting, and the team with the most goals after five attempts is the winner. If it is still tied, the teams continue to alternate shooters until one team has more goals on an equal number of chances.

This tiebreaking system was adopted in 1970. Prior to this, tie matches were either replayed, or sometimes decided by the drawing of lots, which meant the outcome was literally determined by who managed to avoid pulling the shortest straw. The shootout was determined to be a better solution than blind luck.

Two World Cup finals have ended in shootouts. In the United States in 1994, Brazil and Italy were tied at zero, and Brazil won the shootout 3–2. In 2006 in Germany, Italy and France were tied at 1–1. The Italians made all five of their kicks and won the match as David Trezeguet famously hit the crossbar on his attempt for France.

Spanish goalkeeper David De Gea has a long way to go to match the accomplishments of Neuer and Buffon, but the Manchester United star is undoubtedly at the top of the game going into the 2018 World Cup.

The Madrid native played his youth soccer in the system of local La Liga club Atlético Madrid, playing his first match for the senior team in 2009 at age 18. By this time, De Gea had made more than 40 appearances for the national program underage squads, for whom he continued to play while winning the starting job for Atlético. That 2009–10 season, he led Atlético to the UEFA Europa League championship, a competition for top European league clubs that do not qualify for the UEFA Champions League, the premier European club tournament.

FIVE MOST EXPENSIVE GOALKEEPERS
(BY ANNUAL SALARY)

DAVID DE GEA
MANCHESTER UNITED
$13.9 MILLION

SAMIR HANDANOVICH
INTER MILAN
$10.9 MILLION

MANUEL NEUER
BAYERN MUNICH
$8.8 MILLION

THIBAUT COURTOIS
CHELSEA
$8.3 MILLION

JOE HART
MANCHESTER CITY
$7.6 MILLION

EUROPEAN LEAGUE
SINGLE SEASON CLEAN SHEET RECORD HOLDERS

Bundesliga (Germany) 20
Manuel Neuer
Bayern Munich 2014-15

La Liga (Spain) 26
Francisco Liaño
Deportivo 1993-94

Serie A (Italy) 21
Gianluigi Buffon
Juventus 2015-16

Premier League (England) 21
Petr Čech
Chelsea 2004-05
Edwin van der Sar
Manchester United 2008-09

BANK BREAKER Gianluigi Buffon

$47 MILLION

Gianluigi Buffon is the most expensive goalkeeper in history. When the Italian star moved from Parma to Juventus in Serie A in 2001, he commanded a transfer fee of more than $47 million. The move paid off as Buffon led Juventus to seven Serie A titles and was named Goalkeeper of the Decade 2000–2010.

Gigi Buffon is the captain of the Italian national team and has played more than 170 matches in the goal for his country.

In 2010–11, De Gea played so well for Atlético, which finished seventh in La Liga, that both Spain's starting keeper Iker Casillas and manager del Bosque were quoted as saying the 20-year-old was the future starter for La Roja.

After the season, Manchester United courted De Gea, convincing him to leave his homeland for England. The cost was about $28 million, a Premier League record for goalkeepers. De Gea struggled to adjust during his first season in Manchester, but ended the 2012–13 season with 11 clean sheets in 28 appearances as United won the Premier League. He was named to the Premier League Team of the Year for the first of four consecutive seasons.

In May 2014, De Gea was finally named to the senior national team as the third to Casillas and Pepe Reina, and played for Casillas at the end of a friendly victory four weeks later. He was on the team at the 2014 World Cup, but never saw any action in Brazil.

David De Gea's superior skills are so undeniable that Spanish national team manager Vicente del Bosque had no choice but to make him the starter over World Cup champion and team captain Iker Casillas before Euro 2016

De Gea's first competitive start came in a qualifier for Euro 2016 against Luxembourg, which Spain won 4–0. De Gea was named the starter ahead of Casillas for the tournament and kept two clean sheets in two matches as Spain lost to Italy 2–0 in the round of 16.

De Gea kept three clean sheets as Spain went unbeaten in the first five qualifying matches for the 2018 World Cup in Russia. Spain will enter the tournament on the next tier of teams below Brazil, Argentina, and Germany. With the way De Gea has played, he may well be the reason Spain rekindles the magic that led to the glory of 2010.

TEXT-DEPENDENT QUESTIONS:

1. In May of 2009, who made his debut for the German senior team at age 23?

2. In 2001, Buffon moved to Juventus for a goalkeeper record fee of how much money?

3. Name the Manchester United goalkeeper star who is undoubtedly at the top of the game going into the 2018 World Cup.

RESEARCH PROJECT:

This chapter discusses the best current goalkeepers in the sport, but who were the best ever to play the game? Do the research to write a report on the top five players in the history of the position, including stats, style of play, and explain why you think they were the best.

Advantage: when a player is fouled but play is allowed to continue because the team that suffered the foul is in a better position than they would have been had the referee stopped the game.

Armband: removable colored band worn around the upper arm by a team's captain, to signify that role.

Bend: skill attribute in which players strike the ball in a manner that applies spin, resulting in the flight of the ball curving, or bending, in mid-air.

Bicycle kick: a specific scoring attempt made by a player with their back to the goal. The player throws their body into the air, makes a shearing movement with the legs to get one leg in front of the other, and attempts to play the ball backwards over their own head, all before returning to the ground. Also known as an *overhead kick*.

Box: common name for the penalty area, a rectangular area measuring 44 yards (40.2 meters) by 18 yards (16.5 meters) in front of each goal. Fouls occurring within this area result in a penalty kick.

Club: collective name for a team, and the organization that runs it.

CONCACAF: acronym for the *Confederation of North, Central American and Caribbean Association Football*, the governing body of the sport in North and Central America and the Caribbean; pronounced "kon-ka-kaff."

CONMEBOL: acronym for the South American Football Association, the governing body of the sport in South America; pronounced "kon-me-bol."

Corner kick: kick taken from within a 1-yard radius of the corner flag; a method of restarting play when a player plays the ball over their own goal line without a goal being scored.

Cross: delivery of the ball into the penalty area by the attacking team, usually from the area between the penalty box and the touchline.

Dead ball: situation when the game is restarted with the ball stationary; i.e., a free kick.

Defender: one of the four main positions in soccer. Defenders are positioned in front of the goalkeeper and have the principal role of keeping the opposition away from their goal.

Dribbling: when a player runs with the ball at their feet under close control.

Flag: small rectangular flag attached to a handle, used by an assistant referee to signal that they have seen a foul or other infraction take place. "The flag is up" is a common expression for when the assistant referee has signaled for an offside.

Flick-on: when a player receives a pass from a teammate and, instead of controlling it, touches the ball with their head or foot while it is moving past them, with the intent of helping the ball reach another teammate.

Forward: one of the four main positions in football. Strikers are the players closest to the opposition goal, with the principal role of scoring goals. Also known as a *striker* or *attacker*.

Free kick: the result of a foul outside the penalty area given against the offending team. Free kicks can be either direct (shot straight toward the goal) or indirect (the ball must touch another player before a goal can be scored).

Fullback: position on either side of the defense, whose job is to try to prevent the opposing team attacking down the wings.

Full-time: the end of the game, signaled by the referees whistle. Also known as the *final whistle*.

Goal difference: net difference between goals scored and goals conceded. Used to differentiate league or group stage positions when clubs are tied on points.

Goalkeeper: one of the four main positions in soccer. This is the player closest to the goal a team is defending. They are the only player on the pitch that can handle the ball in open play, although they can only do so in the penalty area.

Goal kick: method of restarting play when the ball is played over the goal line by a player of the attacking team without a goal being scored.

Goal-line technology: video replay or sensor technology systems used to determine whether the ball has crossed the line for a goal or not.

Hat trick: when a player scores three goals in a single match.

Header: using the head as a means of playing or controlling the ball.

Linesman: another term for the assistant referee that patrols the sideline with a flag monitoring play for fouls, offsides, and out of bounds.

Long ball: attempt to distribute the ball a long distance down the field without the intention to pass it to the feet of the receiving player.

Manager: the individual in charge of the day-to-day running of the team. Duties of the manager usually include overseeing training sessions, designing tactical plays, choosing the team's formation, picking the starting eleven, and making tactical switches and substitutions during games.

Man of the Match: an award, often decided by pundits or sponsors, given to the best player in a game.

Midfielder: one of the four main positions in soccer. Midfielders are positioned between the defenders and forwards.

OFC: initials for the *Oceania Football Confederation*, the governing body of the sport in Oceania.

Offside: a player is offside if they are in their opponent's half of the field and closer to the goal line than both the second-last defender and the ball at the moment the ball is played to them by a teammate. Play is stopped and a free kick is given against the offending team.

Offside trap: defensive tactical maneuver, in which each member of a team's defense will simultaneously step forward as the ball is played forward to an opponent, in an attempt to put that opponent in an offside position.

Own goal: where a player scores a goal against their own team, usually as the result of an error.

Penalty area: rectangular area measuring 44 yards (40.2 meters) by 18 yards (16.5 meters) in front of each goal; commonly called *the box.*

Penalty kick: kick taken 12 yards (11 meters) from goal, awarded when a team commits a foul inside its own penalty area.

Penalty shootout: method of deciding a match in a knockout competition, which has ended in a draw after full-time and extra-time. Players from each side take turns to attempt to score a penalty kick against the opposition goalkeeper. Sudden death is introduced if scores are level after each side has taken five penalties.

Red card: awarded to a player for either a single serious cautionable offence or following two yellow cards. The player receiving the red card is compelled to leave the game for the rest of its duration, and that player's team is not allowed to replace him with another player. A player receiving the red card is said to have been *sent off* or *ejected.*

Side: another word for team.

Stoppage time: an additional number of minutes at the end of each half, determined by the match officials, to compensate for time lost during the game. Informally known by various names, including *injury time* and *added time*.

Striker: see Forward.

Studs: small points on the underside of a player's boots to help prevent slipping. A tackle in which a player directs their studs toward an opponent is referred to as a *studs-up challenge*, and is a foul punishable by a red card.

Substitute: a player who is brought on to the pitch during a match in exchange for a player currently in the game.

Sweeper: defender whose role is to protect the space between the goalkeeper and the rest of the defense.

Tackle: method of a player winning the ball back from an opponent, achieved either by using the feet to take possession from the opponent, or making a slide tackle to knock the ball away. A tackle in which the opposing player is kicked before the ball is punishable by either a free kick or penalty kick. Dangerous tackles may also result in a yellow or red card.

Throw-in: method of restarting play. Involves a player throwing the ball from behind a touch line after an opponent has kicked it out.

Trap: skill performed by a player, whereupon the player uses their foot (or, less commonly, their chest or thigh) to bring an airborne or falling ball under control.

UEFA: acronym for *Union of European Football Associations*, the governing body of the sport in Europe; pronounced "you-eh-fa."

Winger: wide midfield player whose primary focus is to provide crosses into the penalty area. Alternatively known as a *wide midfielder*.

World Cup: commonly refers to the men's FIFA World Cup tournament held every four years, but is also associated with the FIFA Women's World Cup, international tournaments for youth football, (such as the FIFA U-20 World Cup), and the FIFA Club World Cup.

Yellow card: shown by the referee to a player who commits a cautionable offence. If a player commits two cautionable offences in a match, they are shown a second yellow card, followed by a red card, and are then sent off. Also known as a *caution* or a *booking*.

FURTHER READING, INTERNET RESOURCES & VIDEO CREDITS:

Further Reading:
Perez, Mike. *Lionel Messi: The Ultimate Fan Book.*
London, England: Carlton Books, 2017.
Jökulsson, Illugi. *Ronaldo (World Soccer Legends).*
New York, NY: Abbeville Kids, 2015.
Mattos, Jon. 2014 FIFA World Cup Brazil™ Official Book.
London, England: Carlton Books, 2014.

Internet Resources:

FIFA, www.fifa.com

FC Barcelona: Lionel Messi, https://www.fcbarcelona.com/lionel-messi

Real Madrid: Cristiano Ronaldo
http://www.realmadrid.com/en/football/squad/cristiano-ronaldo-dos-santos

UEFA: Champions League
http://www.uefa.com/uefachampionsleague/

Video Credits:

Chapter 1:
The magic of Messi's dazzling footwork is summarized here:
http://x-qr.net/1FL5

Chapter 2:
Watch Luis Suárez's pivotal moment in the 2010 World Cup:
http://x-qr.net/1Hhy

Chapter 3:
Toni Kroos and Germany dismantle Brazil at the 2014 World Cup:
http://x-qr.net/1Edc

Chapter 4:
Check out this compilation of the skills of Sergio Ramos:
http://x-qr.net/1Dp1

Chapter 5:
Check out this comparison video between Manuel Neuer and Gianluigi
Buffon: *http://x-qr.net/1DvB*

INDEX

INDEX

Andrew Luke

ABOUT THE AUTHOR:

Andrew Luke is a former journalist, reporting on both sports and general news for many years at television stations in various locations across the US affiliated with NBC, CBS and Fox. Prior to his journalism career he worked with the Boston Red Sox Major League baseball team. An avid writer and sports enthusiast, he has authored 26 other books on sports topics. In his downtime Andrew enjoys family time with his wife and two young children and attending hockey and baseball games in his home city of Pittsburgh, PA.

PICTURE CREDITS: